Jord Hollenberg

Rules of origin in the WTO and in other free trade agreements - An overwiew

GRIN Verlag

Bibliografische Information der Deutschen Nationalbibliothek:

Die Deutsche Bibliothek verzeichnet diese Publikation in der Deutschen National-
bibliografie; detaillierte bibliografische Daten sind im Internet über http://dnb.d-
nb.de/ abrufbar.

Imprint:

Copyright © 2003 GRIN Verlag GmbH
Druck und Bindung: Books on Demand GmbH, Norderstedt Germany
ISBN: 978-3-638-92082-7

This book at GRIN:

http://www.grin.com/en/e-book/41007/rules-of-origin-in-the-wto-and-in-other-free-
trade-agreements-an-overwiew

GRIN - Your knowledge has value

Der GRIN Verlag publiziert seit 1998 wissenschaftliche Arbeiten von Studenten, Hochschullehrern und anderen Akademikern als eBook und gedrucktes Buch. Die Verlagswebsite www.grin.com ist die ideale Plattform zur Veröffentlichung von Hausarbeiten, Abschlussarbeiten, wissenschaftlichen Aufsätzen, Dissertationen und Fachbüchern.

Visit us on the internet:

http://www.grin.com/

http://www.facebook.com/grincom

http://www.twitter.com/grin_com

December, 19, 2003

RULES OF ORIGIN

IN THE

WORLD TRADE ORGANIZATION

AND IN OTHER

FREE TRADE AGREEMENTS

AN OVERIEW

by Jord Hollenberg

Rules Of Origin

A. Introduction "The Core Issue of Rules of Origin"

B. Historical Background and Development

C. Methods of Determining Origin
    I. Substantial Transformation
    II. Ad Valorem Percentage Test
    III. Specified Process Test
    V. Change in Tariff Heading Test (CTH)

D. Defining Rules of Origin under GATT / WTO
    I. Non-preferential Rules of Origin
- Dispute concerning the New American Rules of Origin for Textile Products among the European Communities and the United States (WT/DS85; WT/DS151)
        1. The Core of the EC-US conflict
        2. Measures Affecting Textiles and Apparel Products (I); WT/DS85
        3. Measures Affecting Textiles and Apparel Products (II); WT/DS151
        4. Result
    II. Preferential Rules of Origin

E. Rules of Origin as a Trade Barrier

F. Rules of Origin as a Factor of Production

G. Conclusion

References

2

A.   Introduction "The Core Issue of Rules of Origin"

Rules of Origin are methods to extract the origin of a product (and sometimes of services[1]), and help to determine the nationality of an imported good or product. The importance of rules of origin has to be seen in the light of economic values or any kind of trade restriction. Once the origin of a product is known, preferences or restrictions to the product can be much simpler applied by the importing country. Such preferences and restrictions on the imported good are for instance duty-free entry into a Free Trade Area (FTA), quantitative restrictions on goods originating in a country subject to a quota, or anti-dumping duties on goods from the targeted company that originate in the targeted country[2]. Furthermore, rules of origin are also used to compile trade statistics, and for "Made in ..." labels that are attached to products[3].

As long as all parts of a product were manufactured and assembled primarily in one country rules of origin remained an uncontroversial and neutral device. But trade and economy are not under fixed or immovable conditions; thence the rise of multinational corporations and the production of goods in multiple stages, using parts that are produced around the world, enabled rules of origin to be used as effective means of protection and trade barriers. Bearing in mind that goods are produced from different parts around the world and under different free trade agreements, rules of origin do not have one correct definition and vary much in application and function[4].

One of the main objectives of rules of origin should be uniformity and simplicity in their administration. Although this is not always true, developing and developed countries have undertaken the task towards simplification, harmonization and liberalization of rules of origin. This harmonization work has been carried out under the auspices of the Committee on Rules of Origin (CRO) of the World Trade Organization (WTO) and the Technical Committee on Rules of Origin (TCRO) of the Brussels-based World Customs Cooperation Council, which has been

---

[1] Dehousse / Ghemar / Vincent: J.W.T. 36(1): p. 67.
[2] Policy Brief: Rules of Origin: Conceptual Issues, p. 1.
[3] Trading into the Future: "Rules of Origin; made in ... where?", p. 35.
[4] Policy Brief: Rules of Origin: Conceptual Issues, p. 1.

responsible for the technical part of the work, including discussions on the rules of origin options for each product[5].

After all, an Agreement on Rules of Origin (ARO) was established in the WTO. This 'first-ever' agreement is designed to harmonize and to clarify non-preferential rules of origin for goods in trade on the basis of the substantial transformation test. The WTO wants to ensure that their rules are transparent and do not distort or disrupt on international trade, that they are administered in a consistent, uniform, impartial and reasonable manner, and that they are based on a positive standard[6]. That means the ARO in WTO wants to state what does confer origin rather than what does not[7].

B.   Historical Background and Development

Until 1994, GATT had no specific rules governing the determination of the country of origin of goods in international commerce. Contracting parties were free to determine its own origin rules, and could even maintain several different rules of origin depending on the purpose of the particular regulation[8].

Article VIII:1(c) of the GATT Agreement, dealing with fees and formalities connected with importation and exportation, states that "the contracting parties also recognize the need for minimizing the incidence and complexity of import and export formalities and for decreasing and simplifying import and export documentation requirements"; and the Interpretative Note 2 to Article VIII states that "it would be consistent with paragraph 1 if, on the importation of products from the territory of a contracting party into the territory of another contracting party, the production of certificates of origin should only be required to the extent that is strictly indispensable".

It is accepted by all member countries that harmonization of rules of origin i.e., the definition of rules of origin that will be applied by all countries and that will be the same whatever the purpose for which they are applied, would facilitate the international trade flow. In fact, misuse of rules of origin may transform them into a trade policy instrument *per se* instead of just acting as a device

---

[5] Estevadeordal / Suominen: p. 14.
[6] WTO – Trade Policy Courses: at 12.2 (Summary).
[7] USITC: International Harmonization of Customs Rules of Origin, Investigation No. 332-360, Background.
[8] WTO – Trade Policy Courses: at 12.1 (Historical Background).

4

to support a trade policy instrument. Given the variety of rules of origin, however, such harmonization is a complex exercise[9].

In 1981, the GATT Secretariat prepared a note on rules of origin[10] and, in November 1982, Ministers agreed to study the rules of origin used by GATT Contracting Parties[11]. Not much more work was done on rules of origin until the Uruguay Round negotiations. In the late 1980s developments in three important areas served to focus more attention on the problems posed by rules of origin:

First, an increased use of preferential trading arrangements, including regional arrangements, with their various rules of origin; second, an increased number of origin disputes growing out of quota arrangements such as the Multifibre Arrangement and the 'voluntary' steel export restraints; and third, an increased use of anti-dumping laws, and subsequent claims of circumvention of anti-dumping duties through the use of third country facilities. The increased number and importance of rules of origin led the Uruguay Round negotiators to tackle the issue during the negotiations[12].

However, this work was planned to end by 1996. Due to wide divergences between the European Communities (EC) and the United States (US), and, afterwards with developing countries, the WTO was forced to twice postpone the conclusion of the negotiations. Nevertheless, many unsolved items remained to be negotiated before the WTO Ministerial Conference in Doha in November 2001[13].

C.   Methods of Determining Origin

The Kyoto Convention recognizes two basic criteria to determine origin[14]: wholly obtained or produced, and substantial transformation.

---

[9] WTO – Trade Policy Courses: at 12.1 (Historical Background).
[10] WTO – Trade Policy Courses: at 12.1 (Historical Background).
[11] WTO – Trade Policy Courses: at 12.1 (Historical Background).
[12] WTO – Trade Policy Courses: at 12.1 (Historical Background).
[13] Dehousse / Ghemar / Vincent: J.W.T. 36(1): p. 68-69.
[14] The Revised Kyoto Convention is an international instrument adopted by the World Customs Organization (WCO) to standardize and harmonize customs policies and procedures around the world. The WCO adopted the original Convention in 1974. The revised version was adopted in June 1999.

First, the wholly obtained or produced-category applies only to a preferential trading arrangements member, and asks whether the commodities and related products have been entirely grown, harvested, or extracted from the soil in the territory of that member, or manufactured there from any of these products. The rule of origin is met through not using any second-country components or materials. Most countries apply this strict and precise definition[15].

Second, further work or material added to a merchandise in another country must affect "substantial transformation" of the merchandise in order to change the merchandise's country of origin, that means if the merchandise is produced in two or more countries, then its country of origin is the country in which the *last* 'substantial transformation' of the merchandise occurred[16].

I.   Substantial Transformation

However, a precise and universally applicable definition of the concept of 'substantial transformation' does not exist. Some guidance can be found in Annex D.1 of the Kyoto Convention[17]. According to Annex D.1, Definition (c) of the Kyoto Convention "the term 'substantial transformation criterion' means the criterion according to which origin is determined by regarding as the country of origin the country which the last substantial manufacturing or processing, deemed sufficient to give commodity its essential character, has been carried out". In general the substantial transformation criterion says that a good originated in the last country where it emerged from a given process with a "distinctive name, character or use"[18]. But the substantial transformation of a good requires more than just a change in the article; it requires a transformation into a *new and different* article, having a distinctive name, character and use"[19].

The substantial transformation test captures a very simple meaning of origin. This will work for a product originating from one single country. But if a product is not necessarily produced in one single country, the good is a product of the country where it *last* underwent substantial transformation in order to prevent of having multiple countries of origin[20].

---

[15] Estevadeordal / Suominen: p. 4.
[16] Bhala: 'Types of Non-Preferential Rules of Origin': p. 339.
[17] O.J. 175, L 100/1; O.J. 1977, L 166/1.
[18] Anheuser-Busch Ass'n v. United States, 207 U.S. 556, 562.
[19] Anheuser-Busch Ass'n v. United States, 207 U.S. 556, 562, and United States v. Gibson-Thomsen Co., 27 C.C.P.A. 267.
[20] LaNasa: 34 Harv. Int'l. L.J. 381.

Substantial transformation is a very flexible method and allows to evolve and to meet technological change; but its flexibility can also lead to inconsistent origin determinations that undermine the certainty required for strategic planning by businesses. Thus flexibility may be easily misused in a result-oriented manner and can accommodate political pressure for more trade restrictive effects. That means the rule might be converted into a search for the most significant processing, instead of the last substantial transformation. Importers and exporters, as well as producers are required to proof substantial transformation, which is obviously fact-intensive, time-consuming and therefore very cost-intensive[21]. Keeping this in mind, the determination of origin makes the rule even more restrictive and complex and contradicts the aims of the substantial transformation test.

However, the substantial transformation test is required by the ARO; but there are three supplementary criteria on the basis of the substantial transformation test in order to determine the origin of goods that are manufactured in, assembled in, or use materials originating in more than one country:

1. An ad valorem (value added) percentage test;
2. A product specific process, as listing specific manufacturing or processing operations which confer or do not confer origin upon the goods; and
3. A specified change in tariff heading.

Nonetheless, all three criteria are not enumerative to determine the last substantial transformation; they can also be used cumulative[22].

II.   Ad Valorem Percentage Test

The ad valorem percentage test defines the degree of transformation required to confer origin on the good in terms of a minimum percentage of value that has to be contributed from the originating country or of a maximum amount of value that may come from the use of imported parts and materials. That means, if the minimum percentage is not reached or the maximum is exceeded, the last production process will not confer origin[23].

This criterion can be expressed in at least three forms: *import content test* where a maximum allowable percentage of imported parts and materials is needed; *domestic content test* where a

[21] LaNasa: An Evaluation of the Uses and Importance of Rules of Origin, pp. 6-7.
[22] Ghonheim: p. 5.
[23] Vermulst: J.W.T. 26(6), p. 64.

minimum percentage of local value added in the last country where the product was processed is needed and; *value of parts test* where originating parts must reach a certain percentage of the total value of parts to confer origin[24].

Generally, the ad valorem method is very simple and precise, but on the other hand it causes many disadvantages. The method ignores exchange rate risks and fluctuations in the price of raw materials. While the status of goods can change on a daily basis, compliance costs und uncertainty for companies may arise. Therefore this test is in general unsatisfactorily[25].

III. Specified Process Test

The specified process test is also referred to as a technical test[26]. This implies a concrete industrial operation. Therefore, to determine origin is to specify "substantial transformation" which occurs when a specific production process has been carried out. That prescribes a certain production or sourcing process that may (positive test) or may not (negative test) confer originating status[27].

The specified process test serves as a useful supplement because is has the advantages of transparency, predictability, and less subjectivity. Additionally, it is the least costly method of determining origin[28].

But the specified process test is not a satisfactory primary test to determine origin because it would be very difficult or almost impossible, to define a process test for the wide range of products made, and further to update these rules for new products and technological advances in production[29]. Hence, the specified process test can also be subject to discretionary protectionist pressures from some concerned industries, because the drafters and administrators of this test have to rely on information upon these industries[30].

---

[24] Ghonheim: p. 7.
[25] Maxwell: 23 Geo. Wash. J. Int'l L. & Econ. pp. 671-672.
[26] Vermulst: J.W.T. 26(6), p. 74-75.
[27] Vermulst: J.W.T. 26(6), p. 74.
[28] Ghonheim: p. 8.
[29] LaNasa: An Evaluation of the Uses and Importance of Rules of Origin, p. 9.
[30] Ghonheim: p. 8.

IV.   Change in Tariff Heading Test (CTH)

The CTH test determines the origin of a good by specifying the change in tariff heading of the Harmonized System (HS) of Tariff Nomenclature. The advantages of CTH are its conceptual simplicity, its ease of application and its lack of discretion. Additionally, the adoption by most countries of the HS will usually lead to uniform determinations of origin in such countries[31]. But the HS is primarily designed as a dual-purpose commodity classification and statistics system and can therefore not always function as an appropriate standard. Additionally, the CTH requires in-depth knowledge of the HS from exporting country administrators and producers / exporters, especially regarding the finished product and the raw materials[32].

D.   Defining Rules of Origin under GATT / WTO

The question arising is how rules of origin can be defined in the WTO. Art I:1 of the ARO states: "Rules of Origin shall be defined as those laws, regulations and administrative determinations of general application applied by any Member to determine the country of origin of goods provided such rules of origin are not related to contractual or autonomous trade regimes, leading to the granting of trade preferences going beyond the application of Art I:1 of the GATT 1994".

This definition implies that two categories of rules of origin exist; both are generally known as non-preferential and preferential rules of origin.

I.   Non-preferential Rules of Origin

The WTO Agreement on Rules of Origin applies to non-preferential rules of origin used in commercial policy instruments such as the application of Most Favored Nation (MFN) treatment under GATT 1994 Articles I, II, III, XI and XIII; anti-dumping and countervailing duties; safeguard measures; origin marking requirements; discriminatory quantitative restrictions or tariff quotas[33].

- **Dispute concerning the New American Rules of Origin for Textile Products among the European Communities and the United States (WT/DS85; WT/DS151)**

In 1996 a serious dispute arose between the European Communities and the United States regarding a change in the US legislation for the determination of the origin of some textiles and

---

[31] Vermulst: J.W.T. 26(6), p. 73.
[32] Vermulst: J.W.T. 26(6), pp. 73-74.
[33] OECD, Moise: TD/TC/WP(2002)33/FINAL, 8.

clothing products[34]. EC producers saw the US modification as a violation of the international rules. On their request the European Commission began a Trade Barrier Regulation[35].

The complaint about the US rules of origin on textiles has to be seen in an essentially new perspective. This litigation lightens a fundamental trade question where it remained rare until now[36].

1.   The Core of the EC-US conflict

Trade in textile products was not one of the free-trade principles of GATT 1947. Thus was hardly prevented by many, inter alia the United States, which was among the hardest proponents of a protectionist policy in that field, because the US textile industry was a grant of employment; especially for less-skilled US workers. But the textile sector was one of the first sectors in which developing countries chose to invest[37]. Beginning in the mid-1950s, those countries increased their exports to the markets of developed countries. To avoid this competition the United States took protectionist measures that resulted in bilateral export restraint arrangements with Italy and Japan, such as the 1961 "Short Term Agreement on Cotton Textiles" (STA), the 1962 "Long Term Agreement" (LTA), or the 1975 Multifibre Agreement (MFA). GATT was asked to enforce theses agreements[38]. Those agreements took a large part of textile trade outside the scope of the GATT, and albeit the legality of these measures was doubtful, they remained unchanged under the limited dispute settlement mechanism of GATT 1947[39].

Because of the decrease of the credibility of the GATT the Uruguay Round negotiations developed the Agreement on textile and clothing (ATC). A 10-year phase-out, ending in 2005, of all specific trade restraints imposed on imports in the textile and apparel sector was implemented[40].

---

[34] WT/DS85/1.
[35] OJ 1996, L 349/71, modified by Regulation 356/95 CE (OJ 1995, L 41/3).
[36] Dehousse / Ghemar / Vincent: J.W.T. 36(1), pp. 68-69.
[37] Dehousse / Ghemar / Vincent: J.W.T. 36(1), p. 69.
[38] Dehousse / Ghemar / Vincent: J.W.T. 36(1), p. 69.
[39] Dehousse / Ghemar / Vincent: J.W.T. 36(1), p. 70.
[40] Baghi: J.W.T. 28(6), pp. 31-42.

2. Measures Affecting Textiles and Apparel Products (I); WT/DS85

The US introduced changes to its rules of origin for textile and apparel products, which entered into force on July, 1, 1996. Some of these rules, in particular the rules contained in Section 334 of the Uruguay Round Agreements Act and implemented through customs regulation, adversely affected exports of EC fabrics, scarves and other flat textile products to the USA. As a result of this change, EC products were no longer recognized in the USA as being of EC origin and lost the free access to the US market that they enjoyed before[41].

The Submission of Previously Freely Exported Products to Quotas

Because of the new US rules of origin, European producers were suddenly faced with a change from free exports to the USA, as being now subject to quotas. According to the pre-1996 legislation the printing and dyeing of clothes was sufficient to originate as a product of an EC member state. Under the new set of rules, the fabric has to be woven in the EC to be considered as originating in one of the member states. For example, a fabric printed and dyed in the EC, but woven in Egypt, whose exports were subject to US quotas, were now considered as being of Egyptian origin and were subject to the quotas allowed to Egypt. Consequently, exported European textile products to the United States were de facto restricted[42].

The Labeling problem

Another consequence of the new rules of origin arose from labeling of silk accessories, such as scarves and foulards[43]. Foulards printed in Italy[44] were considered originating form Italy under the pre-1996 legislation, and a "Made in Italy"-Label was attached. The new rules instead required a "Made in China"-Label, as it is now originating in China, where the fabric was woven. As a consequence, the new labeling was less appealing to American consumers and has therefore a restrictive effect on European textile producers.

First WTO Dispute Settlement Procedure

The EC took the decision to challenge the new American rules of origin in the WTO[45]. The new WTO dispute settlement system requires that conflicts between WTO members must first be

---

[41] WT/DS85/1.
[42] Dehousee / Ghemar / Vincent: J.W.T. 36(1), p. 75.
[43] WT/DS85/1.
[44] Italy is an example for any EC member state, compare WT/DS85/9.
[45] WT/DS85/1.

subject to a conciliation procedure, known as the *procès-verbal*. If the litigants cannot agree on an acceptable solution, a panel of experts will be charged with the resolution of the conflict. In this dispute, the litigants did not go any further than the *procès-verbal*.

Arguments

The arguments invoked were based on Article IV:2 of the ATC and on the ARO.

(a) Article IV:2 of the ATC

The EC argued that the changes were not in conformity with the obligations of the US under the WTO ATC. Article II:4 of the ATC requires that no new restriction in terms of products or Members shall be introduced; and Article IV:2 also prescribes that the introduction of changes in the implementation or administration of restrictions notified to the WTO shall not: upset the balance of rights and obligations between the Members; adversely affect the access available to a Member; impede the full utilization of such access; or disrupt trade under the Agreement. The EC's opinion was that the change in US rules of origin caused precisely those effects and that the US should have initiated consultations with the EC prior to the implementation of such changes, in accordance with Article IV:4 of the ATC.

(b) The ARO itself, and Article 2 ARO

Although the ARO, which provided the elaboration of uniformed rules of origin for non-preferential trade relations, was adopted at the end of the Uruguay Round negotiations, those arguments could not be invoked for some reasons. The harmonization process had to be finished for July, 20 1998; but no result could have been reached during this delay. Although a new deadline had been set in 1999, it has been breached. In fact, the dispute arose at a moment where no uniform rules of origin were applicable.

Furthermore, the EC questioned the compatibility of the changes in US rules of origin within the scope of Article II of the ARO, which contained disciplines that a member must abide by when changing its rules of origin during the transitional period. These disciplines prescribe, inter alia, that "...(b) the rules are not used as instruments to pursue trade objectives, directly or indirectly, (c) they shall not themselves create restrictive, distorting or disruptive effects on international

12

trade, (...) and (e) they are administered in a consistent, uniform, impartial and reasonable manner". The EC was of the view that the new US rules of origin do not respect such requirements.

The Procès-Verbal

During the procès-verbal the US noticed that the new legislation was a breach of Article 4:2 of the ATC. But the US and the EC reaffirmed to cooperate together in the textile sector closely. They committed themselves to achieve a mutually satisfactory resolution in this case[46]. Hence, no dispute settlement panel was needed *(supra)*.

The US commitments

With respect to the EC's request that the US return to the rules of origin set forth in 19 C.F.R. 12.130 for dyed and printed textile and apparel products, the US accepted to amend the US litigation (§ 3 of the *procès-verbal*). According to § 2 the US proposed that the timing and framework for such a legislative change should be after the conclusion of negotiations in respect of the WTO harmonized rules of origin, scheduled for July 20, 1998; and the US committed to propose to Congress its prior rules of origin for silk accessories, silk fabrics, dyed and printed cotton fabrics, dyed and printed man-made fibre fabrics and dyed and printed vegetable fibre fabrics in the context of those WTO rules of origin harmonization negotiations, not later than two months from July 20, 1998[47].

In order to facilitate the trade flow among the EC and the US, the US made three further commitments in § 6 of the *procès-verbal*:

1. European silk scarves and fabrics were allowed to be marketed with an appellation equivalent to "designed in (a Member State of the EC)" in order to make European silk products more attractive on the American market.
2. Different categories of cloths originating in Egypt, Turkey, Thailand and Indonesia were no longer under quantative restrictions and textile visa requirements.
3. The US also promised to take the necessary procedures to remove from quota coverage a couple of printed fabrics from Malaysia, Indonesia and Thailand[48].

---

[46] WT/DS85/9.
[47] WT/DS85/9.
[48] WT/DS85/9.

The EC commitments

In exchange the EC committed to suspend the case and not to refer the dispute to the WTO Dispute Settlement Body (§7 of the *procès-verbal*)[49].

Conclusion

The EC and the US mutually agreed in July 1997 and notified the Chairman of the Dispute Settlement Body on February, 11, 1998.

3. Measures Affecting Textiles and Apparel Products (II); WT/DS151

According to the mutual agreement reached in WT/DS85, on July, 30, 1998 a bill was submitted to the US Senate in order to amend the rules of origin of textile products[50]. Congress adopted the bill setting out special rules of origin for certain textile products:

- fabric of silk, cotton, man-fibre or vegetable fibre should be considered to originate in the country in which the fabric is dyed and printed if at least two of the following finishing operations are preformed in such country: bleaching, shrinking, fulling, napping, decating, permanent stiffening, weighting, permanent embossing or moireing.
- silk accessories should be considered to originate in, and be the growth of, the single country in which the fabric for the accessory is cut into parts and assembled into a completed good. If the fabric of a silk accessory is not cut into parts and assembled in a single country, it shall be considered to originate in the country in which the fabric for the accessory originates.

The first rule saw comeback of the "four operations rules", but only for fabrics.

The EC did not agree that this new US rules were sufficient and they considered that the US had not implemented its commitments *(supra)* in order of being consistent with the US obligations under WTO rules by implementing such new rules. Furthermore, the EC had three major problems with the new set of rules; first, concerning silk accessories; second, concerning finished products such as bed linen and third, concerning a new production technique of yarns, called 'devorage'.

---

[49] WT/DS85/9.
[50] 105th Congress, 2d session, S. 2394.

14

First, in order to determine the country of origin of silk accessories the old US legislation required that they were dyed and printed in the originating country. But the new rules considered as the country of origin the country in which the cloth was woven, e.g. China. In so far that solution did not change compared to 19 USC §3592.

The second problem dealt with finished products such as bed linen, which were not covered by the amendment. They remained subject to the 1996 rules that required a fabric to be knitted or woven in order to originate in one country. The situation was quite ambiguous and unrealistic; i.e., a fabric woven in China but dyed, printed and finished in Italy would have been of Italian origin, where as the same fabric which might have undergone additional processes, like being cut and sewn to produce a tablecloth, would have been originating from China, as it was the country where the fabric was actually woven.

This result was utterly unsatisfactory for European textile producers and Commission tried to reproach the US Administration to introduce specific exceptions in the legislation, instead of a general "four operation rule" for all textile products. Technical proposals were made and the right to request WTO consultations if the amendments were not correctly enacted was invoked.

Nevertheless, the US legislation remained unchanged on that regard. The amendments proposed by the US administration were rejected by Congress. And, the change in the marking legislation concerning "Designed in Italy"-Label was not successful either.

However, the EC was of the opinion that the US had not fulfilled its obligations resulting from the procès-verbal (supra). Where as the US was confident with its new set of rules of origin and argued that their obligation under §3 and §6 of the procès-verbal was to submit these propositions to the Congress immediately in order to launch the process.

Finished products such as bed linen, made of silk accessories, silk fabrics, dyed and printed cotton fabrics, dyed and printed man-made fibre fabrics and vegetable fibre fabrics (see §2 of the procès-verbal) were excluded from the scope of this procès-verbal. Hence, the US administration considered its obligations as being fulfilled. The EC argued the contrary; products referred to in §3 of the procès-verbal were the dyed and printed textile and apparel products mentioned at the beginning of §2 of the procès-verbal.

Third, the European textile producers invented a new production technique of yarns, called "devorage". Devorage is a melting process that creates one single fibre out of two. It was argued that this technique is a substantial transformation to the fibres. As a result it should have been held sufficient to determine origin in that country where it takes place. But this technique has never been considered by the US legislation. It was therefore incorporated in the discussions under the WTO harmonization work of rules of origin.

According to §7 of the *procès-verbal* the EC postponed the formal conclusions in the WTO regarding the commitments of the US. The US never established such rules. Therefore the EC reserved the right to revive the consultations in the event the US do not introduce and enact the necessary legislative amendments.

The second Agreement

Both disputing parties reached a new agreement. The solution set forth in the attached procès-verbal of August, 16, 1999, which has been implemented pursuant to Section 405 of the Trade and Development Act of 2000 entitled "Clarification of Section 334 of the Uruguay Round Agreements Act" as enacted by the US on 18 May 2000[51], modifying 19 USC 3592.

This amendment introduced a §2B and C in 19 USC 3592.
According to the new §2B:

> "Notwithstanding §1C, fabric classified under the HTS as of silk, cotton, man-made fiber(s), or vegetable fiber(s) shall be considered to originate in, and be the growth, product, or manufacture of, the country, territory, or possession in which the fabric is both dyed and printed when accompanied by two or more of the following finishing operations: bleaching, shrinking, fulling, napping, decating, permanent stiffening, weighting, permanent embossing, or moireing."[52]

§2B however stands for a comeback of the 'four operations' rule. Fabrics will be considered as originating in the country where they underwent final transformation. Compared with the pre-1996 legislation only one difference exists, fabrics made of wool are excluded from that general rule.

---

[51] 66 Fed. Reg. 21, 660; WT/DS151/10.
[52] WT/DS151/10.

According to §2C:

> "Notwithstanding §1C, goods (such as handkerchiefs, bed lines, curtains, furnishing articles and cushions) except for goods classified therein as of cotton or of wool or consisting of fiber blends containing 16 per cent or more by weight of cotton, shall be considered to originate in, and be the growth, product, or manufacture of, the country, territory, or possession in which the fabric is both dyed and printed when accompanied by two or more of the following finishing operations: bleaching, shrinking, fulling, napping, decating, permanent stiffening, weighting, permanent embossing, or moireing."[53]

§2C excludes certain cotton products from the scope of the exception. Only silk, vegetable or man-fibers products are able to benefit form the 'four operations' rule. The other products are still subject to the general rule and will be considered as originating in the country where the fabric was woven

Conclusion

Under this new and very complex set of rules of origin wool products remain excluded. They will be originating in the country where they are knitted or woven. Silk, man-made fibres or vegetable fibres products will originate in the country where the four operations took place. The same applies to cotton and fibre blends containing 16 percent or more by weight of cotton products, if not otherwise listed. They will therefore originate in the country in which the fabric was woven and remain subject to quantative restrictions.

4.   Result

Albeit this new set of rules does not solve every problem, most problems concerning the quantative restrictions applied to the goods undergoing their final transformation in the EC are now resolved. They are considered as originating in the EC. Furthermore, the labeling problem has been resolved. 'Made in EC or similar' labels can be attached to the product.

Thence, a satisfactory solution has been found for the EC.

II.   Preferential Rules of Origin

Even though preferential rules of origin are not covered by the ARO of the WTO, a common declaration in Annex II to the Agreement WTO members agree to observe the same principles

---

[53] WT/DS151/10.

when they use rules of origin to determine whether goods qualify for preferential treatment. Preferential rules of origin are used to determine whether certain products originate in a preference-receiving country or trading area, and hence qualify for the trade preference[54].

E.   Rules of Origin as a Trade Barrier

As far as rules of origin are divided into two categories, known as preferential and non-preferential rules, preferential rules of origin are used to determine whether certain products originate in a preference-receiving country or trading area and therefore qualify for the trade preference. On the other hand, non-preferential rules of origin are used for all other purposes, including enforcement of product and country specific trade restrictions that increase the cost of entry (i.e. antidumping duties) or restrict or prevent market entry (i.e. quotas)[55].

As for the trade flow between the contracting parties themselves, rules of origin are not intended to affect the volume of trade in favor of one of the partners to a preferential regime[56]. But rules of origin can be used as a barrier to trade[57], for example to increase trade barriers towards non-contracting parties, and to attract investment into the markets of the contracting parties[58]. Because of determining whether a product originates in a preference-receiving country or trading area, and thereby enters the importing country on better terms than products from the rest of the world, preferential rules of origin allow governments to discriminate between products from different countries. This is a result of the GATT principle of non-discrimination in GATT 1994 Art. XXIV and its most favored nation clause in GATT 1994 Art. I[59].

Countries have created various trading agreements that give preferential treatment to developing countries and regional trading partners. By varying the severity of the required transformation and by allowing different degrees of cumulation on a regional, donor, or global basis, countries use the rules of origin to control the degree of preference. If the preferential rules are formulated in a way that they require a greater transformation of the product than the

[54] OECD, Moise: TD/TC/WP(2002)33/FINAL, 14.
[55] Policy Brief: The Use of Rules of Origin as Barriers to trade, p. 2.
[56] Hirsch: J.W.T. 36(2), p. 178.
[57] Policy Brief: The Use of Rules of Origin as Barriers to trade, p. 2.
[58] Hirsch: J.W.T. 36(2), p. 178.
[59] Policy Brief: The Use of Rules of origin as Barriers of Trade, p. 2.

rules of origin otherwise would require they may serve as a discriminatory policy device that restricts trade[60].

F.   Rules of Origin as a Factor of Production

Rules of Origin are an important factor of production. While certain country-specific or group-specific preferences and restrictions exist, rules of origin have an immediate impact for businesses on profit. Therefore it is essential to analyze the different rules of origin, to quantify their cost, and to treat them as factor of production in determining where to source their investments, purchase raw materials, produce or purchase intermediate materials, and assemble their final products[61].

Because businesses have an interest in determining whether quotas or similar measures bar the entry to a desired market trade restrictions and preferences have an immense impact on cost of goods and may hinder the entry of a good into a country. It is obvious that a profit-maximizing business will buy the cheapest product if it is of equal quality. Therefore, such measures as tariffs and quotas must be included in the cost calculations for the good in determining where to buy or produce a good[62]. But those measures are only two of many; businesses try to sell their products where it enjoys further preferences such as cheap labor, the level of labor skills, transportation costs or, probably more important, the size and the potential of the preferential market[63].

Regarding these factors it is not surprising that rules of origin are mostly employed as a strategic instrument i.e. in the North American Free Trade Agreement (NAFTA) and in the EC member states. Both are major economies and offer remarkable sized markets, as well as many trade concessions.

Therefore, by detecting a location where a good receives the most beneficial treatment of production and by seeking for those benefits in countries where the good will be sold,

---

[60] Policy Brief: The Use of Rules of origin as Barriers of Trade, p. 2.
[61] LaNasa: An Evaluation of the Uses and Importance of Rules of Origin, p. 4.
[62] LaNasa: An Evaluation of the Uses and Importance of Rules of Origin, pp. 4-5.
[63] Hirsch: J.W.T. 36(2): p. 180.

19

businesses could minimize the trade restrictions and maximize the trade preferences placed on that good.

G.   Conclusion

Rules of Origin always remained a very complex task. Although the WTO took a step towards harmonization and transparency of rules of origin by implementing a first-ever agreement on rules of origin in WTO, they almost only regulated the application of non-preferential rules. Preferential rules of origin are only mentioned in Annex II of the ARO and can still be used for protectionist measures towards third countries.

Keeping this in mind and reviewing the cases dealt with in this thesis, one cannot deny that even non-preferential rules of origin are not always free of protectionist measures, e.g. the United States measures affecting textiles and apparel products from the European Communities. However, a dispute arising on rules of origin does not necessarily mean that a panel will decide it. Parties can agree on a conciliation procedure, known as the *procès-verbal* and can therefore prevent a panel of the dispute settlement body.

Therefore, the harmonization of rules of origin is not always the best solution; it can only be a second choice. As long as countries differentiate between restrictions and preferences they allow to certain countries, and as long as these countries are seeking for economical success and growth, rules of origin will remain controversial and unfortunately inefficient.

Therefore, the harmonization process of rules of origin is not finished yet.

References

1. Bhala, Raj: 2001.International Trade Law: Theory and Practice, 2nd edition. Note on Non-Preferential Rules of Origin, 'Types of Non-Preferential Rules of Origin'

2. Dehousse, Franklin, Katelyne Ghemar and Philippe Vincent: 2002. "The EU-US Dispute concerning the New American Rules of Origin for textile Products."
   Journal of World Trade 36(1).

3. Estevadeordal, Antoni, Kati Suominen: 2003. Rules of Origin in the World Trading System.

4. Ghoneim, Ahmed. "Rules of Origin and Trade Diversion: The Case of the Egyptian-European Partnership Agreement."

5. Hirsch, Moshe. 2002. "International Trade Law, Political Economy and Rules of Origin: A Plea for a Reform of the WTO Regime on Rules of Origin."
   Journal of World Trade 36(2).

6. International Center for Economic Growth: Policy Brief, Free Trade Agreements and Rules of Origin, Rules of Origin.
   Brief#0012

7. LaNasa, Joseph. 1995. "An Evaluation of the Uses and Importance of Rules of Origin, and the Effectiveness of the Uruguay Round's Agreement on Rules of Origin in Harmonizing and Regulating Them."

8. LaNasa, Joseph: Rules of Origin under the North American Free Trade Agreement: A Substantial transformation into Objectively Transparent Protectionism,
   34 Harv. Int'l. L.J. 381.

9. Maxwell, Michael: 1990. Formulating Rules of Origin for Imported Merchandise: Transforming the Substantial Transformation Test, 23 Geo. Wash. J. Int'l L. & Econ. 669.

10. OECD; Moise, Evdokia: The Relationship Between Regional Trade Agreements and Multilateral Trading Systems, Rules Of Origin, TD/TC/WP(2002)33/FINAL.

11. USITC: International Harmonization of Customs Rules of Origin, Investigation No. 332-360

12. Vermulst, Edwin: 1992. Rules of Origin as Commercial Policy Instruments – Revisited, Journal of World Trade 26(6).

13. Trading into the Future, 2nd edition, Revised, March 2001.

14. WTO – Trade Policy Courses 12 "Rules of Origin".

Cases:
1. Anheuser-Busch Ass'n v. United States, 207 U.S. 556, 562 (1908).
2. United States v. Gibson-Thomsen Co., 27 C.C.P.A. 267 (1940).
3. WT/DS85.
4. WT/DS151.